Barcelona.

Long [...] dinners and even later drinks a [...] in the Catalan capital. A tranqu [...] with a rich cultural scene has b [...] travellers for years.

The city has a rich cultural history, from Gaudi and Miró to Picasso. But unlike certain other European cities where high rents have flushed out artists, the art scene here manages to remain dynamic.

To say Barcelona is re-inventing itself would be wrong. Its art, culture and food scene are deeply rooted in its past. Even the street art in Poblenou has clear influences in the bright colours of Gaudi's Park Güell.

But it's the people who shape the city. We spoke to gifted personalities: an artist and designer couple, a key figure behind Sónar festival, a local culinary expert and a boundary-busting musician. Our picks are complemented by a graphic art showcase, a piece of flash fiction and a feature story by local talents. It's all about original minds and the creative vibe. Get lost in the sights, sounds and flavours of the city. Get lost in Barcelona.

This park used to contain La España Industrial, Barcelona's biggest mill. As most industrial buildings in Barcelona, the space got abandoned, but, with the help of the council, transformed in the mid 1980s into a public space. Whether you want to go for a picnic, a paddle, a jog or a game of football, this vast open space is littered with relics that remind you of its past use, and features a gigantic dragon sculpture by the Catalan artist Andrés Nagel. And if this isn't enough to tickle your fancy, turn admire the classic works of Manuel Fuxà, José Pérez Peresejo and Antoni Alsina.
• Parc de l'Espanya Industrial, Carrer de Muntadas, 1-37, Sants

Grey-haired women exchanging the latest news from the neighbourhood, men enjoying their first cerveza of the day— markets are an inspiring way to feel the heartbeat of a city. In Barcelona the vibrant and original feeling can be found in the smaller district markets, such as in Sants or Gracia. Discover the rich variety of Catalan products from Arbequina olives to Xató sauce and, if you don't live here, ask yourself why most of these indigenous products never reach your own fridge in London, Berlin or Paris.
• Mercat de la Llibertat, Gracia, mercatsbcn.com

From Broad Beaches to Futuristic Housing

Més Que Una Ciutat

This apartment is located in *Casa Bloc* in Sant Andreu and considered a symbol of the rationalist architecture that flourished in Barcelona during the Second Republic (1931–1939). Happily, 1/11 has lately been returned to its initial 1939 state. The 60-square-metre area is furnished with original pieces like the Thonet Mundus chair and a Marcel Breuer dining table—making it like some sort of time capsule. The place is open for visits on Saturday.
• Casa Bloc, Sant Andreu museudeldisseny.cat

Outdoors | **Pool with a View**

Originally built in 1929, and made popular during the 1992 summer Olympics, *the municipal pool of Montjuic* offers one of the best views of Barcelona and a great place to escape the summer heat. Spotted by creative directors of advertising agencies all over the world, it has served as the backdrop to Kylie Minogue videos and countless TV commercials. Fearless leapers can get the best view from the top of the the 25 metre-high diving board.
• Piscina Municipal de Montjuïc, Montjuïc, esports.bcn.cat

Shop **Technicolour Dream**

Chile-born interior designer *Jaime Beriestain* has set up his contemporary shop just south of Diagonal, selling a wide range of hand-picked products ranging from furniture and accessories to books and flowers. His wares share up the city's aesthetic style of bold colours and graphics. And the in-store restaurant has become a magnet for the local fashion crowd.
• Jaime Beriestain, Eixample, beriestain.com

Outdoors **Platja, Playa, Beach**

Barcelona is one of the rare European metropolises boasting access to the Mediterranean. Unfortunately, those swimming in the waters within walking distance from the city might end up encountering a dead rat, a used condom or a syringe. If those are not your idea of sunken treasure, head east to the beaches of *Montgat Nord*, 25 minutes from Plaza Catalunya by train, to enjoy clean sandy beaches with the Barcelona skyline safely in the horizon.
• Playa Sant Joan, Montgat

Food **Grapes and Greatness**

Cañete's kitchen is the centre of its two flanking restaurants and an institution in Barcelona. Although this place is the favourite of celebrities like DJ Richie Hawtin don't come expecting a fancy VIP atmosphere. Though it belongs to those with a more elevated touch, the locale remains unpretentious and down to earth—like most of Barcelona's restaurant scene.
• Cañete, El Raval, barcanete.com

10

Culture | Welcome to Utopia

In 1973 Ricardo Bofill found an abandoned cement factory from the 1920s on the outskirts of Barcelona and transformed it into his studio and private living space. Within the former eight silos, the imaginative architect created plain concrete rooms where surreal elements are mixed with Catalan gothic decorations. The complex is surrounded by eucalyptus, palm, olive and cypress trees. With such a magical atmosphere, the headquarters of "Taller de Arquitecturea" are considered to be one of the finest offices worldwide. *The Factory* can be visited by request if you are working in any field related to architecture. No less spectacular, the neighbouring building is easier to access: *Walden 7* is a social-housing experiment incorporating Bofill's view on modern residential architecture. Its alien-style design, a vertical labyrinth over 16 stories with seven interconnecting interior court-yards, two rooftop pools and gardens, has a deep connection with B. F. Skinner's science-fiction novel "Walden Two", in which he depicts a utopian community. In fact, the house holds a vibrant collection of more than 400 residences. A volunteer of the community will be happy to show visitors around—if they apply two weeks in advance. Lastly, the 102-metre-high chimney restored by Alfredo Arribas has an observation point on top. Those with vertigo might want to stay on the ground or come face to face with its transparent floor and ceiling. It houses the circular restaurant *El Mirador de Sant Just* and rewards one's expedition of curiosity with a 360-degree view of The Factory and Walden 7.

• Various locations, see Index p.67

Emma Pardos & Michael Swaney
They're in love with each other
and with the city of Barcelona.
Emma's eponymous bag label
showcases designs that stand
out for their sophistication,
yet maintain a playful approach.
Meanwhile, Michael is an artist
who abides only by his own
norms. The works he produces
are best described as "Art Brut"
(a term coined by French artist
Jean Dubuffet in the 1940s).
This trend proclaims freedom
in art while eschewing traditional
standards and expectations
of beauty

Emma Pardos & Michael Swaney, Designer and Artist

Love at First Sight

While Barcelona definitely has plenty to offer, not every proposition is worth delving into—sometimes a little selectivity is required. Whether it's modern or traditional food, alcoholic or refreshing drinks, hot clubs, attractive shopping destinations, places to just relax and hang out or sightseeing spots, Emma Pardos and Michael Swaney are savourers of all levels. They take us on a tour through the best corners of their hometown

Emma, what is so enthralling about Barcelona that keeps you here and prevents you from living somewhere else?

Emma: It has the perfect climate and size. It's a city that's easy to get around and blue skies are very common.

You are originally from Kimberley, Mike. Since when have you lived in Barcelona and what made you move here?

Mike: I've been here for 9 years now, but initially came here 12 years ago for the first time on a gut instinct with the idea that it would be the perfect place for me. I was attracted to the word "Barcelona" and to how I imagined the city. And then I met Emma...

So it was love at first sight?

Mike: It definitely was. This city buzzes with an energy that I have yet to feel someplace else. The fact that the Mediterranean is close by, the palm trees, the density of the city and how easy it is to get around, the sun light and short winters, the food, its distinctly different neighbourhoods, the people, the history.

Do you remember your first impression of the city?

Mike: I remember it just feeling very exotic and historic and rich in personality. I can remember this distinct tropical smell in the air at the airport and I still get it every time I return from a trip. I think I told my friends and family about being amazed at how people seemed to take a second to enjoy the simple things in life, like having a coffee while sitting in the sun.

Where do you live in Barcelona?

Emma: The Gracia neighbourhood, as we had an opportunity to renovate an apartment exactly the

way that we wanted. It's a really central area yet without the overcrowding present in the centre of the city. And, above all, it's less touristy. It's very well connected and has a great atmosphere. There's everything you need here. It's like a little town.

Mike: There's a lot of young people and young families in Gracia. But there are also people who've lived here their whole lives. There are lots of specialty shops for pretty much everything you need and tons of restaurants and bars. We love going to a bar that is just below our place called *Vinilo*. There's another cool bar nearby called *Raïm 1886*.

Emma: There's a ton of very beautiful antique furniture shops, clothing shops and cinemas.

Every big city has a few "hip" areas. What is the "hippest" neighbourhood in Barcelona at the moment?

Emma: That would be El Born, which is part of the Ribera neighbourhood. It's one of the most central neighbourhoods in the city where most of the city's independent designer shops have been located for a couple of decades. Although it's not as central, another neighbourhood which is getting more and more popular is Poblenou although it's not as central.

What is so special about El Born?

Emma: It's a very old neighbourhood, close to the sea, with very narrow streets. It's full of shops, restaurants, bars and it's where the *Picasso Museum* and *Santa Maria del Mar* are located. Also, the *Palau de la Música Catalana*, which is a modernist style building. Its magical interior will convince you to enjoy a concert there.

14

Oscar Tusquets and Carles Díaz redesigned the interior of the Palau de la Música Catalana in the 1980s

Cosmo
Eixample

Bilbao
Gracia

La Estrella
El Born

Bar Bodega Quimet
Gracia

La Flauta
Gracia

Betty Ford
El Raval

Which are the places to be in this neighbourhood?
Emma: If you want something to eat, *Bar Pasajes* or *Bar Mundial* are great for tapas. For a night time drink, *Pony Café* or the cocktail bar *Gimlet*. This neighbourhood is full of bars to choose from anyway, so you can't really go wrong.

What is your favourite venue in Barcelona for a nice breakfast?
Emma: For late risers, at 10am you can go to *Cosmo* and have a good coffee or freshly squeezed juice, cake or a good sandwich... It's also a recommendable place to go at any hour of the day, not just for breakfast.

And lunch?
Mike: *Bilbao* on Carrer Perill in the Gracia neighbourhood has a nice three-course menu. Also *La Estrella* in the Born serves great food if you are looking for something more Mediterranean.

What do you recommend for dinner?
Mike: *Bar Bodega Quimet* in the Gracia neighbourhood. You can eat some tapas and charcuterie in a great atmosphere. *La Flauta* is another really good spot for a wide range of tapas. And *Betty Ford* in the Raval neighbourhood is a great place to eat a hamburger and fries and to have a drink at night.

Homemade liqueurs top the counter at Bar Bodega Quimet, which boasts an authentic atmosphere and good kitchen

Regarding traditional Barcelona cuisine, what's your favourite and which venue does it best?

Mike: We love to eat tapas. You can go to *La Cova Fumada* in the Barceloneta neighbourhood, *Bar Mundial* in the El Born neighbourhood or *Velódromo* in the Eixample neighbourhood.

Emma: A really common drink is vermouth and there are many different so-called "cellars", or bodegas where you can have one. Like at *Vermutería del Tano*, *Bodega Marin* in the Gracia neighbourhood, *Bar Calders* in the Sant Antoni neighbourhood or *Morro Fí*. Another really good, non-alcoholic drink to try between meals is "horchata". It's made from tiger nuts, water and sugar. At the *Horchateria Sirvent* in the Sant Antoni neighbourhood you can even have one to go.

What's the ideal place to go and relax?

Mike: Our rooftop is great though we only seldom take advantage of it. We live in a gorgeous plaza with a clock tower in the middle and look over the terraces below. I love going up to Montjuic, El Carmel or Parc Güell to take in the views of the city and the sea in the distance. In the summer, we leave the centre to go to beaches on the outskirts of the city.

Imagine you were to create an artwork titled "Barcelona". What would you do, Mike?

Mike: I would do a massive mural mosaic or a sculpture. Or I might just make a big park full of sculptures, mosaics, pillars and buildings.

Emma, if you needed to design a product absolutely essential for Barcelonans as well as for tourists, what would it be?

Emma: The thing I've learned over the years is that bags in Barcelona have to have a zipper and they need to be crossbody bags. Those are the things that someone living in Barcelona wants for a bag.

As a designer you surely must have a critical view on fashion. What are your favourite stores?
Emma: There's now a circuit of different shops with their own brands and local designers' products near Carrer Brosolí. Places like *La Tercera*, *Colmado*, *Ivori* and others. Then you've got *Colmillo de Morsa* on Carrer Flassaders 12 that has its own brand and clothes by local designers. There's also the area around the Paseo del Born where there are a lot of clothes shops.

What about vintage wares?
Emma: If you like vintage there are a lot of beautiful shops in the centre around Raval neighbourhood. Also, you can find furniture shops throughout the entire city. Els Encants Vells is an essential place that you should not pass up. It's a morning market on Mondays, Wednesdays, Fridays and Saturdays. You can find a bit of everything there. The Mercat de Sant Antoni is open on Sunday mornings and there you can basically find books, photos, stamps etc. You should also try the flea market that takes place once a month.

Are there stores that sell your bags?
Emma: Yes. *Nuovum* on Carrer del Pintor Fortuny, *Colmillo de Morsa* on Carrer Vic 15 and Carrer Flassaders 12, as well as *Madam PumPum* on carrer Bonavista 16.

What is your favourite gallery?
Mike: *ADN* Galeria.

And museum?
Mike: Probably the *Picasso Museum* but the *Museu de Cultures del Món*, the museum of world cultures, that opened recently seems like it could also be really cool.

Is there a bookstore that you recommend?
Mike: *Múltiplos* is a great art book shop and so is *La Central*.

Imagine you have a guest coming over to Barcelona for a weekend. How would you spend the time?
Emma: The secret to Barcelona is to walk around the city. We would eat breakfast in Gracia or Rambla Catalunya and afterwards walk towards the centre via Paseo de Gracia and visit La Pedrera or La Casa Batlló. Once we got to Las Ramblas, we could walk around that area as it's full of shops; the *MACBA* and the *Mercat de la Boquería* are good places where we would eat lunch. Later we could walk over to El Born and have a coffee there. Then we could walk to the Barceloneta neighbourhood and see some emblematic places near the market, the *Mercat de la Barceloneta*, and have some good tapas or just enjoy the views by the sea side. The second day, we would recommend going to one of the many panoramic view points of the city. One of them could be the *Montjuic Castle.* from which you can see the sea, the port full of colourful shipping containers and a panorama of the city. We could also take a walk around Montjuic while we're up there and where there's several museums including the *Joan Miró Foundation* and the *MNAC*. There's also the *Jardines del Teatro Griego* (Greek Theatre Gardens) that you can easily visit.

El Born

Crossroads

Still in the centre but not as crowded as the Barrio Gotico—this is a district with many faces. The labyrinth of alleyways hosts young designers' studio stores alongside bars that have existed here for decades

Food | Houses of History and Taste

Traditional locations with an authentic atmosphere and homemade food—El Born still has the good old gems: *Bar Mundial*, for example, is an institution here. It was founded in 1925 and has been run by the same family over many generations. The furniture is Catalan style, the walls are filled with vintage pictures of legendary boxers. The bar is famous for the tasty tapas and is always crowded. The specialities of the house are "Navajas a la Plancha", "El Filete con Foie y Salsa de Frutos del Bosque" and the delicious giant dessert tray. Another traditional place for a quick bite in

an informal dinner setting is *Bar del Pla* (pictured). Chef Jordi Peris has been responsible for the food in the recent years. He presents tapas with a modern twist—but remains rooted in tradition. Just two blocks down you'll find Casa Mari y Rufo, an unassuming hole-in-the-wall run by a family of food-loving Catalans. Duck in through the hanging jamón and settle into a cozy backroom, where you'll be urged to try the navajas, octopus and, if your group is large enough, steak cooked over a hot stone. Take heed.

• El Born, various locations, see Index p.67

A Good Wind

You won't find any flamenco aprons or garish Gaudí coasters here. Instead you'll discover linen espadrilles, handwoven baskets, Marseille soaps and rustic knives. These are just some of the hand-crafted goods sold at *Bon Vent*, a concept store dedicated to the breezy, Mediterranean lifestyle. The shop's wooden organic displays will likely send you adrift to a rustic home in a seaside village. You might pick up a pair of traditional Abarcas—handmade Spanish shoes made with a jute sole. Here, the simple things are the finest things.
• Bon Vent, Carrer de l'Argenteria, 41, El Born, bonvent.cat

Food Inclusive Lunching

Upon taking a seat here one immediately feels that this is not just another coffee shop. Old stones decorate the walls and bring out the colourful furniture. The menu is filled with international food: all artisanal, organic and fair trade products. A special coffee shop: a place where social action and cultural diversity are at the forefront. Besides the food, visitors can take part in activities like art exhibitions or photography workshops. The terrace is half-covered, making the setting perfect at any time of the year. *Espai Mescladis* is a local meeting point due to its lunch menu that changes daily.
• Espai Mescladis, Carrer Carders, 35, El Born, mescladis.org

Food Fisherman's Friend

This simply furnished place looks like a traditional pescadería at first sight. Fresh fish lie around on ice with labelled prices per kilo and a fishmonger behind the counter. But on the side of the counter is an open canteen-style dining room with a dozen tables. The system of local mini-chain *La Paradeta* is simple: choose your fish directly at the counter and how you want it prepared. You then get a number to be called when your plate is ready. The place takes no reservations and as the quality is high and the prices very affordable, make sure to come early in the day to avoid disappointment.
• La Paradeta, Carrer Comercial, 7, El Born, laparadeta.com

24 Hour Funky People

Somewhere to go both before your party on Saturday and after the party on Sunday—and it's no rave. *Guzzo Club* is an institution for acid jazz, Afro, soul, funk and Latin tunes. In the afterparty slot on Sundays from noon, DJ Fred Guzzo brings in his records for the "Brunch Club". Cocktails and food are accompanied by a funky live jam. If you still have energy from the night before, this is the perfect way to spend it. It might also be a good occasion to bring the little ones and entertain them with your moves—as the event is family friendly.
• Guzzo, Plaça Comercial, 10, El Born, guzzo.es

Food **New Style**

This recently launched restaurant, offering creative tapas in an exquisite but casual setting, belongs to Eva Arbonés and Fran Heras, who used to work at El Bulli and Arola. *Llamber* is located in a former fruit warehouse in front of El Mercado del Born that still retains some of its original elements. The famous signature tapas here are "Croquetas" and "Buñuelos". Reservations are advisable, because the best seats are near the open kitchen where guests can observe the creative process of preparing the delicacies from below.
• Llamber, Carrer de la Fusina, 5, El Born, llamberbarcelona.com

Food **The Saigon-Barça Connection**

Just in front of Bar Mundial lies *Moskito Tapas*, where Catalonia suddenly ends and you find yourself in Vietnam. Beers from all over the world and excellent homemade dumplings are the essence of this place, which fits the profile of an Asian-style bar. The atmosphere is always a bit chaotic and most of the time this small location is crowded with a young audience. This might just the only place in Barcelona where they serve thick, strong and sweet Vietnamese-style coffee.
• Moskito Tapas, Carrer dels Carders, 46, El Born, mosquitotapas.com

Shop A Walk of Craft and Fashion

Born is full of unique fashion and local design. Take, for instance, *Iriarte Iriarte* (pictured), a studio and showroom where natural leather bags and accessories are designed and handcrafted by Iriarte herself. The elegant bags are individually numbered as to show the uniqueness of each piece. On the upper floor of this tiny studio is *Après Ski*, a workshop that produces a line of accessories by Lucía Vergara. All her products are sold as limited edition only. Just around the corner you will find the label *About Arianne*: Ariadna Guirado and Ernest Vidal are the creative minds behind this local footwear brand. They produce their stock in La Rioja, famous for craftsmanship in leather. Round the next corner and to the left watch out for another tiny doorbell. Ring it to reach the atelier-shop of *Natalie Capell*. Its dark, theatrical atmosphere makes it look like a location from a Tim Burton movie. Capell's luxurious and elegant dresses—each piece is unique—are on display here. High-fashion lovers could also head to *Coquette* on Carrer Rec; the women's boutique stocks local designers with international brands like APC or Isabel Marant. In the same street, close to Mercado Princesa you'll find *Room*, a cosy shop with a Mediterranean feeling and a selection of vintage and local fashion.

• El Born, various locations, see Index p. 67

The Voice of Sónar

Georgia Taglietti
She is an Italian native and head of communication and international media & press for the Sónar festival. As one of the key people involved in organising the festival she has been welcoming artists from around the world since 1995. It's no wonder her contributions helped transform Sónar into one of the most ambitious events on the global festival circuit

Georgia Taglietti came to Barcelona in 1985 and witnessed the city's metamorphosis from a sleepy local scene into an internationally renowned tourist destination. LOST iN talks to Georgia about this transformation, her enlightening experiences with Sónar festival and some of her most treasured places in Barcelona

You were born in Italy. When did you come to Barcelona and what were the reasons?

From the age of three we spent our holidays in Cadaques, a wonderful spot on the Catalan coast where Dalí lived. It was a great place, very international. There I learned lots of languages and I became bilingual in Spanish. My best friend at the time was the daughter of one of the core founders of the Journalism and Advertising Faculty of Barcelona Autonomic University. So to move from Brescia in Italy to Barcelona has been quite simple for me. We had lots of friends living in Barcelona already. This was back in 1984.

How did you first get into music and when did you decide you wanted to make your career in music?

My family was always musically oriented. My father was a traveller; he loved music, especially jazz. So it's in my blood. I went to concerts when I was really young, jam sessions and so on. I never decided though to make a career in music, it just happened by chance 20 years ago.

You have been part of the Sónar festival since its launch in 1994— if you were to describe all those years alongside a local festival that emerged as a global player what would you say?

It has been a long great journey through the electronic music culture. For us, as well as the Sónar directors, the transformation of Sónar has always been a very thoughtful and cautious one. I am lucky to work with people who are at the same time both visionaries and practical down-to-earth entrepreneurs. So I recall the years we have spent together as an endless learning process, and it's still this way right now. A global player does not stop evolving. This is the secret of being there after so many years.

What was it like living in Barcelona in 1984 or 1994? What was different back then compared to today and how did it inspire you to do what you do?

Barcelona was a very different city back in 1984. I had a great time and it was a provincial yet wild place to live. There was a lot going on in terms of clubbing, culture, an explosion of architecture, design, music and theatre, before the Olympics came and put Barcelona on the tourist map. The 1992 Olympics was a game-changer in terms of tourism, but not in terms of creativity. So I guess what I always loved about Barcelona was the size of the city and its quality of life. Though Sónar happened in the years after the 1992 in which optimism and internationalism conquered the city, and both were important factors to support the birth of a private initiative such as Sónar was and is. Barcelona is the home of Sónar—and Sónar gives back a lot to the city in terms of content and business.

How closely linked is the history of the Sónar festival to the history of town?

Barcelona and Sónar have a story together because Sónar was an urban festival from the very beginning. I think Sónar has put Barcelona in the centre of the electronic culture map, it has helped build the cultural tourism that a city needs in order to be perceived not only as a sightseeing spot, but as a cultural incubator.

What would be your general advice for someone coming to Barcelona for a weekend?

Oh well, to walk around Barcelona is the best, starting in La Barceloneta, Born, and visiting the new El Poblenou neighbourhoods that are blooming with new places every day. There are a lot of good food spots, bars and cafes, and some nice weekly events with street food and design markets happening...

How do you see the cultural art and music scene of Barcelona nowadays? And where can a visitor best experience it?

El Poblenou is certainly an interesting spot to check the pulse of the city in terms of new entrepreneurs and ideas, as well as Raval. In El Poblenou around the Vila Olímpica and Diagonal Mar areas many artists have converted the former factories and warehouses into lofts, galleries, and shops, making the area known as a creative outlook. I personally think that there is more need for promoters than artists. The lack of promoters and venues makes the cultural art and music scene quite invisible.

At the moment what are the juiciest Barcelona city districts and why?

As I mentioned, Sant Antoni is becoming one of the most interesting, as they renovate the area around Parallel. We still don't know what it will look like but it will definitely change the look and feel of the district. And again Le Poblenou is certainly alive and kicking.

What is your favourite district and what makes it special?

El Born, the rambling district below the Old Town. I am a classical person. It is still chic and interesting and you can still find interesting bars, restaurants and stylish boutiques that have nice ideas.

What are your current top five stores in Barcelona?

Baluard is the best bakery in Barcelona, outstanding and worth queuing for as it is in the heart of La Barceloneta. The *Les Topettes* store in the El Raval district, is very nice too. It is a perfume store in the middle of Raval dedicated to the art of pampering with amazing rare fragrances, exotic hand creams and exquisite moisturisers. I also have to recommend the *MiiN Korean*. The store devoted to Korean beauty. They have really great, hard to find unique products for beauty fans like me! If you like books the *Libreria Calders* is a fantastic bookstore in the middle of the buzz of the Sant Antoni neighbourhood bars. And for one-off souvenirs I have to suggest the sweet *The Only Fish in the Sea* store. The store is a poem owned by wonderful Maria and it is devoted to marine objects, beautiful jewellery and unique accessories.

Can you please recommend two up and coming Barcelona based artists who deserve attention?

The fashion designers *Colmillo de Morsa* and the online illustrator's gallery of Mirilla Works.

Can you name your favourite restaurants and tell us what makes them unique?

Meneghina restaurant is a very special and romantic place where you can enjoy an Italian family cooking very high quality food. My favourite couple manages it. The chef is from Napoli and the host, his wife is from Barcelona. They serve fantastic Italian food in the cosiest place. I love to eat my

The city of Barcelona is a city of ambiance, flavour and wine... Meneghina has all of them in abundance

Koyshunka
El Gòtic

Gresca
Eixample

Guzzo
El Born

Sunday lunch there. If you like Japanese food the *Koyshunka* restaurant is amazing. It is my favourite Japanese restaurant in Europe. And if you are curious about Catalan cuisine you have to go to *Gresca* restaurant in Calle Provenca. Here, one of Barcelona's up and rising chefs—again a fantastic person—Rafa, is running one of the most interesting, new restaurant spots in the town!

Bar or club: what are some of your favourite places to hang out in Barcelona?
   Guzzo is the spot I go so often I won't count the times. It is a bar, and a club. They play soft jazz and funk, they serve really great cocktails, the decoration is my cup of tea and I love the hosts. So this is my place.

If someone gave you a fortune and you had a weekend to splurge it in Barcelona, what would you do?

A Spa at the Mandarin Oriental. Then some shopping at Paseo de Gràcia. After that I would rent a boat in the port, invite all my friends for a great boat party or possibly buy myself a venue and become a promoter! Or most realistically give all the money to the Banc dels Aliments foundation—which is probably what I really would do. Consumerism does not make us happy.

And, finally, can you give us an example of something that you haven't done in Barcelona but have always wanted to so far?
   Running the annual marathon. I have done pretty much everything else I wanted to so far.

Tale of Two Cities

A Charnego in the Kingdom of Custo
by Eugenia Rico

The first song I learned was a song in Catalan. It was called
"Baixando la font del gat" ("Going down the Cat's Fountain".) My
grandfather, who had learnt it when he was a prisoner during
our Civil War, taught it to me. My grandfather was a prisoner in
the Montjuic castle and he fell in love with Catalonia.

He would always talk of it as of the Promised Land where all
the masías (Catalonian farm houses) had a paved road. Years later,
during my first trip to Barcelona, I thought of how charming such
a land should be so that a war captive could fall in love with it in the
midst of hunger and bombings. My grandfather walked all the way
to France in a chain of prisoners. Once there, they were put against
the wall, told the war was over and that they were to be shot; but
just then, an official black car with a small Catalonian flag stopped
over and the man who got off it ordered the firing squad to stop
because too much blood had already been shed for Spain. Grandfather was saved thanks to illustration, modernisation and the

famous "seny" (common sense) which had been the Catalonian bourgeoisie's brand for so long.

Thus, I already loved Barcelona before arriving in it for the first time from France, where I was enjoying my Erasmus student exchange scholarship. Nowadays, when I visit Barcelona on a weekly basis by AVE, the high-speed train that connects in two hours the two most different and most comparable cities in Spain, I think that the right way to see Barcelona for the first time is the way I saw it: approaching it from Europe and not from Madrid. Speaking English with my friends from Berlin in the Born neighbourhood cafés, we were answered in Spanglish. Now and despite the fact that the ride between Madrid and Barcelona lasts a little more than two hours, I feel as if Barcelona was closer to New York than to Madrid.

I came to participate in a Kinfolk event. There's good food, nice conversation and live elegant music in the background. All quite similar to so many meals shared at dinner or lunchtime in the Malasaña or La Latina neighbourhoods in Madrid, except its name, for the "kinfolk" events take it from a magazine based in Portland, Oregon—one of the brands who play a part in a city that loves to create new trends. Such a thing in Madrid would be impro-visation, whereas here it's marketing. A group of friends who get together to enjoy "slow food"—except those friends are everybody and they don't know each other. I talk to people, they come from London, Milan, even from Crete.

Piero is from Rome. "Barcelona is architecture, Madrid is people", he tells me. "Madrid is the capital city of Spain, Barcelona is the city the whole world takes as the capital of Spain."

From my first visit to Barcelona I am crazy for "pan tumaca"—a simple piece of bread with olive oil, tomato and garlic which, for me, is the essence of Mediterranean pleasure. The waiter who serves it speaks Catalan to me and I respond in Spanish.

"I arrived by the AVE this morning, that's why I don't speak Catalan", I utter.

"Well, you should have learnt it by now", he responds.

He is not joking. So I continue the conversation in Galician, my mother tongue and another official language of the country.

"Hey mate! I can't understand you. It's better if you speak Spanish."

"Exactly", I say, "we need to have a common language, if you don't want me to speak Spanish, how about English?"

"I do prefer English, it's just that I don't speak it" he says and insists once again that every Spaniard must speak Catalan even if he or she has just got off the AVE. Despite that, we have already become friends.

"You are quite nice for a 'charnega'", he says.

It is not quite clear what a charnego exactly is. It is clear that I am one. It is a derogatory word used to name those who are not from here. Some believe it only refers to natives of Barcelona whose parents are from other regions of Spain. Juan Marsé climbed to the Olimpus of "charnega" literature with pieces such as "The Bilingual Lover". I'm proud of being a charnega and I'll tell you why: The word was coined by people of the Low French Pyrenées neighbouring the border area of La Garrrotxa to designate children of French and Spanish mixed couples. It is derived phonetically from the French pronunciation of the Catalan word "xarnera" which means hinge, charniere in French for defining the situation of children from families of two nationalities. I am proud of being a hinge, a bridge, an Asturian, half Galician, from the third planet of the Solar System who loves Barcelona and Catalonia.

I have always thought that nationalism can be cured by travelling and that is why I am meeting my friend Marion, a classmate of mine from The Free University of Brussels and a professor at Catalonia's most important private university. She has her views about the latest developments in town.

"Catalonia is still a very rich region but it is no longer the richest one, the Catalonian politicians are the only leaders in Europe who did not lose public estimation due to the recession because they accused Spain for all the problems and people believed them. All the bad things that happen in Barcelona are not their fault, it is Spain's fault. In Madrid people fight for saving public health care and education, here people fight for independence." Marion takes me to a Poetic Brothel, a session in which they recite poetry right into your ears, one of these things you can find in the neighbourhood of Borne in Barcelona. We bump into Pau there. My friend Pau is a supporter of the independence idea. "It is like leaving your parents' home", he says. Barcelona has grown up and it's time for it to stand for itself.

"The difference is that you can always go back to your parents' house, if you leave Spain you won't be able to return.", I tell him. "Barcelona may be most beautiful city in Spain but Madrid is the most welcoming. In Madrid everybody's from Madrid after spending only an hour there, it doesn't matter where one was born. There are many Catalonians in Madrid, people from Barcelona have good positions in the central administration and they are kindly received. Here it is practically impossible to work in public administration if you are not a Catalonian. I am pro-independence because that will make us even. We, the rest of the Spaniards, would not have any rights in Catalonia, just like it is now, and the Catalonians would not have any rights in Madrid, just the opposite to current situation." says Montse Pau's girlfriend.

Later on, at the Paralell Theatre, I attend the premiere of a Spanish speaking play by Pablo Alvarez performed in Spanish at the peak of the pro-independence demonstrations, called "Microporn for Money". At some point in the play the main character exclaims: "Parla catala s'ils plau" ("Speak only Catalan please").

"But your mother is from Seville!", she is told by another character and the public roars in laughter.

"We are all charnegos around here", my friend Carles tells me, "our parents come from different parts of Spain just the same way that there are Catalans all around Spain. I used to be pro independence till I have started travelling around the world, when you come back from India, Barcelona seems to be clearly a Spanish city, maybe the most beautiful among Spanish cities but it still more similar to Madrid than New Delhi, Paris, London or Berlin."

The nationalists are dangerous, they drove Europe into the WWI and they could drive Barcelona into foolishness.

"If you become independent I would like to ask for political asylum", I say, "Barcelona is my favourite city in Spain, the city where I would like to write and grow."

"It is a mere distraction, the politicians prefer to talk about independence rather than give up millions of Euros they have stolen", says Montse, "They don't want independence, they want more money.

And I think that as long as we can talk with both humor and serenity over an "arroz negre", while Barcelona keeps being the city of dialogue, while we can understand each other with a unique Mediterranean culture look, I can feel at home here despite the pro-independence demonstrations. The rest of the Spaniards would like Barcelona to love us just as we love it.

"In Madrid people talk about the recession, in Barcelona people talk about Madrid" concludes Montse. And we all concentrate on the millenary wisdom of rice, Barcelona's culinary symbol which, long time ago, was a "charnego" dish brought from China.

Eugenia Rico is a Spanish novelist and journalist. She has won several awards including the "Ateneo de Sevilla" and the "Premio Espiritualidad". She was the first Spaniard selected as a "Writer in Residence" at the prestigious Writer's Workshop, University of Iowa. The Madrileña travels to Barcelona weekly

No Boundaries

Sergio S. Vidal
He is a creative who fits no ordinary mould. As an art director he has worked in Stockholm and Berlin. As a musician he travels the world. Together with Pablo Bolivar they form "Pulshar". The sound of the Barcelona-based duo is released under Loco Dice's prestigious label "Desolat". Just like Sergio, their music follows no conventional pattern; it tackles styles from dub to techno. Sergio also runs a record label called "Avantroots"

Drawing from his experience in urban culture, Sergio shares his rich knowledge about the local scene in Barcelona. As a musician, producer and DJ he is deeply rooted to the city's club culture: he knows where to buy the hottest records in town, where to listen to the latest talents on stage and—of course—where to party until dawn

You have lived in Madrid, Berlin and Stockholm. Why did you come back to Barcelona in 2010?

I moved from Barcelona to Berlin, but I kept my flat in Barcelona—"just in case". I needed a change, but at the same time I didn't want to forget Barça because my friends, my label and my band were there, and I was still deeply in love with the city. It was like when you temporarily break up with your girlfriend. You know it won't be forever, but you just need some time to think. Barcelona is special for me mainly because of the sunlight and the weather. It may sound obvious or basic, but when you are outside of BCN you don't miss the party or the restaurants as much as you miss the natural mood of the city. You miss the breeze, the rays of light that filter through the streets of Ciutat Vella, going to the beach by motorbike and walking down Via Laietana till the end, vermouths in Raval at lunch time, enjoying the city views from Montjuic, or taking a walk in Barceloneta at night. It's like the city is a person in itself, like a close friend who's always in good mood. And if it was a person, Barcelona would be a woman, no doubt.

You are deeply connected to the graphics as well as to the music scene. Some people would argue that Barcelona does not have a big underground scene... Would you say this is true?

Well, the word "underground" doesn't have the same meaning right now as it did 10 or 15 years ago. The underground thing is massive and trendy now, and there are a lot of people who call things "underground" that are not underground anymore. So after this clarification, I would say that there is no such scene, because the people here work in a very

independent and individualistic way. At the same time we could say that there are a lot of people involved in things like music, design, art, skate, tattoo, bikes and nightclubbing that make the city alive in some ways. But the "real" underground is not easy to find, because most things in Barcelona are now targeted towards foreigners or tourists. You have to dig to find special and authentic places.

And if you do dig—where can you find places in town which represent subculture?

On my list there are record stores like *Subwax* for electronic, dub techno, *Discos Paradiso* for electronic, african music, reggae, *Wah Wah* in Raval for 1960s, Rock, Funk, Soul, Psych and *Lost Tracks* in Gracia. For going out I would recommend *Foxy*, a rock and house bar in Raval, the art space *Espai Niu*, also with live acts and Djs in Poblenou, the clubs *Loveless* and *Switch* and the classic *Moog Club* in Raval for techno. Worth mentioning are the rock and skate fiestas "Movin'On" with Soul, Funk and Northern Soul or *Bombón*, a latin bar, and *33/45*, also in Raval. Talking about galleries and museums: I would say the *Centre d'Art Santa Mònica*, *Hangar* and *Niu* are the most interesting.

As a music lover, where can I hear the most innovative sound in Barcelona?

I think Barcelona still needs places to listen to electronic music outside of the party or dance scene context because I think most of the innovative electronic music is happening outside of these scenes. But, for example, the art space *Niu* has real alternative activities, among them DJ and live sessions that feature local and new artists.

Also, you can listen to good electronic music in the *33/45 Bar*... and the guys from Monkey Bar have shows and really good taste with their parties.

You work in different creative fields. Where in town do you get your inspiration? And where do you find peace?

I guess I get inspiration in my own space but when I want to relax I usually go to Montjuic. I think it's because I used to practice Kung Fu there in a place close to Font del Cat. I have so many nice memories from there that I always associate that place with good vibes. Also in Montjuic there is a place called *La Caseta del Migdia* where you can sit and relax outside the city centre and take in amazing views of the harbour. Poblenou also has nice places to walk and chill. For example, the *Poblenou Cemetery* is a special place for me.

What is the best soundtrack for strolling around in Barcelona on a sunny day?

I have a playlist called "Smoke Raps" with Devin The Dude, Curren$y, Schoolboy Q, Snoop and Those Guys—you know, a Cali feeling which fits perfectly with Barcelona. But also I like the cloudy days there, and in that case, I'd choose some dub electronic stuff.

Which is the building you like most in town and why?

Casa Milá (La Pedrera) is maybe too obvious, but the first time I was inside I felt things, aesthetically, that I had never felt before. There are so many incredible small details in every place of that house. Probably, though, I would choose the building made for the *Joan Miró Foundation*.

Oh, good choice. The building is by Josep Lluís Sert, who worked with Corbusier. And if that building were a song...

It would be something luminous but mathematic at the same time. It could be "Tedra" by Kenny Larkin.

In Barcelona everyone famously has one too many drinks. Where would you send a party animal on his or her last night in town?

Well, I like to start at lunchtime around 1pm, the vermouth time. I think that in order to prepare for partying, you should eat well beforehand. So we can start in Barri de Sants—it's not fancy, but it's real and cheap. My fave bar there is *El Capritxo* on Melcior de Palau in Sants where the owners give you free fresh fish with every beer and the ambience is really "motivational". You can continue in Poble Sec or Raval where you can find a lot of bars of every kind. I'm sure you'll find lots of original, funny and strange people to chat with all day. If your budget is more than ok, I would stop for dinner in the Italian restaurant *Xemei* in Poble Sec but you should book days in advance. After dinner, you can go to a good gig in *Sala Apolo* or any other interesting event. Also, it's good to ask people for suggestions, because the best alternative parties and after parties usually are not in Time Out. So, if you stay in the club until the end, usually 4:30 or 6 in the morning, I'm sure you'll have met someone who knows someone who is having an after-party at home. If you are lucky, you will enjoy an after-party in a flat with a terraza— that's heaven. If you don't want to or can't sleep, you should go to Barceloneta, and lay in the sand or take a splash in the beach if the weather is nice. Then it's up to you to continue another day.

Both the Joan Miró Foundation (above) and Sala Apolo (below) can lead to romance, but it is mostly a question of taste

Direct Flight to BCN

A Showcase by Sergio S. Vidal

Photographer, graphic artist, musician... Many talents, many names—from his background in graffiti culture Sergio is also known as "Aphro". His photographic perspective towards the urban life in Barcelona as well as his surreal collages are sourced from this heritage

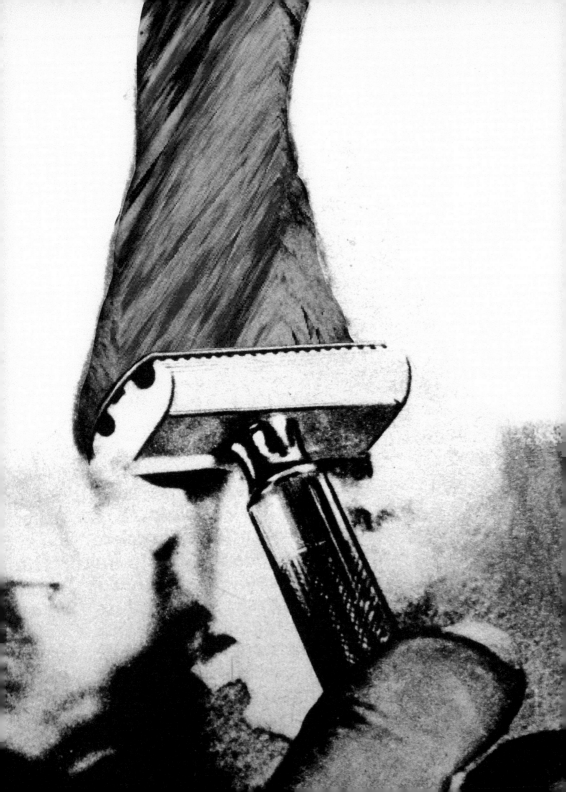

Suzan Taher
She is a food expert and blogger.
She was born in the Middle East,
studied in Paris, lived in Berlin
and London where she received
a diploma in "Food and Wine"
from Leiths. Now Suzan has been
living with her family in Sitges for
a few years. In her blog "Foodie
in Barcelona" she reviews
restaurants on a weekly basis

Suzan Taher, Food Expert

Creative Heritage

In recent decades Barcelona's chefs have played a major role
in Europe's Champions League of culinary art. But the days of the
exclusivist experiments à la El Bulli are over. The latest evolution
of the city's gastronomic life is in down-to-earth concepts, accessible
to a wider audience. Creativity is still the major force behind this
process, but tradition is also highly valued by the younger chefs

New school: La Publilla (above)—famous for local food with a modern twist. Old school: The Fideuada at Xiringuito Escribà (below)

As a foodie, which traditional dish should I not miss in Barcelona and where can I get it?

Calçots season is pretty special, you find yourself an outdoor bbq or go for a Calçots menu at one of the restaurants around the city. They look like green onions and are grilled on the embers with skin, dirt and all. Then you slide off the skin and dip them in a homemade Romesco sauce. And try not to get it all over your clothes.

Where else in Barcelona can I taste a dish that encompasses the city's spirit?

My favourites include *Morro Fi* and *Casa Martino* in Sant Antoni. The croqueta is a universally loved snack and they are everywhere. Or a tortilla, if it has an alarmingly wet centre, it's spot on.

As someone who also likes to try strange food... What should I order?

Catalan dishes are not really strange, they have simply preserved a way of eating that is foreign and eccentric to a generation that has grown up eating chicken breast. Tripe is a favourite, as are stuffed pig feet and stewed calf's head. Snails are still very popular and are usually sold by poultry merchants. Then there is a dish called Mar i Muntanya that combines every-thing: rabbit, snails, fish and prawns.

What about tapas culture? Could you explain the concept? Are there different styles of tapas restaurants? Do you have a recommendation?

The Catalans are a gregarious and social bunch. And they also eat late, especially in the summer, which means they start feeling a bit peckish around the time when the rest of Europe is having dinner. You have a choice between a tapa, Pintxo—usually served on a toothpick, or a montadito—a miniature open sandwich. There are so many choices in Barcelona, most people just go to one of their local restaurants. Stand out places include *Quimet Y Quimet*, which specialises in canned foods and montaditos, and *Cerveceria Catalana* that has an impressive selection and is always busy. I would also mention *Tapas 24* off Passeig de Gracia and *Taperia Lolita* in Sant Antoni.

So, let's move away from tradition... What are the latest trends in the Barcelonan restaurant scene? Where can I experience them?

There are many Mexican restaurants and taquerias around and new ones are always opening: from affordable places like *Tamarindo* to high-end ones like *Hoja Santa*. There are also plenty of classy Peruvian restaurants around such as *Pakta* and also affordable places like *Ceviche 103*, where you can get a complete lunch menu for 15 euros.

After several years of lobbying against the bureaucrats, a fledgling food truck and street-food market scene is finally emerging. Although there are many organisers, from the publication "BCN Mes with Eat Street" to the guys at Paolo Alto Market, every time there's a market that's open, it is crammed with people and the food is great. Stands like Reina Croqueta and Caravan Made achieve excellent traffic.

Are there markets worth going to other than the famous Boqueria?

The Boqueria is great but it's overrun with tourists on food tours and I feel like one third of it has been transformed into stalls selling fruit juices. Every area in Barcelona has its own market, most have a few markets. In Gracia, for instance, you have the *Mercat de la Llibertat* and *L'Abaceria Central*. Both are favourites of mine.

Where are your favourite restaurants if you have a night out with friends and why?

Out of all the Albert Adria places, *Tickets* is my favourite one. If you can get a table there, you will have a great experience. If you can't, then I recommend going across the street to *Espai Kru* from the Iglesias brothers—who are the principal backers of Adria. Its main focus is raw fish and it isn't the same crazy style as *Tickets*, but the prices are great and so is the quality. *La Pubilla* in Gracia serves the best value meals in town with lighter interpretations of Catalan dishes. It is totally informal and always buzzing—a lot of fun. If I am in the centre of town and I want to go somewhere with friends but I haven't made a reservation, I opt for one of the Tragaluz places. Either *Cuines Santa Caterina* by the Santa Caterina market or *Bar Lobo*. They are on the pricey side and I generally abhor restaurants that use those annoying remote control terminals to punch in your order instead of good old pen and paper. But the cooking is consistent, the spaces are nice and they usually have a table available.

Which bars do you hit after dinner?

Casa Almirall in the Raval because they just don't make places like this anymore. The *360 Terrace*, there are many options with a view in Barcelona but I like this one's location in the Raval. *Xixbar Gins and cocktails* which has over 100 gins to choose from.

Barcelona is also famous for its weather. What are the restaurants with a view or nice terrace you would recommend?

Barraca in Barceloneta and its sister restaurant *Barracuda*, in Castelldefels, serve great rice dishes and seafood, but it's not going to be cheap. Some say that you can get the best rice in town at *Kaiku*. If you are looking for something more old school, try *Xiringuito Escriba*.

What is the best present that I can buy here and take home?

The canned seafood is pretty spectacular and the myriad of varieties they have here are very hard to find abroad, such as: marcona almonds, tomato marmalade, smoked paprika and, finally, salsa espinaler—so that you can spike your crisps and recreate that Vermouth experience.

That all sounds great! Is there anything that you don't like about Barcelona?

The bureaucrats, but they are awful anywhere. Apart from that, the Barcelonans are probably my favourite people in the world. The three things they say the most when you speak to them are: "No pass nada"—everything's fine, "no te preoccupies"—don't worry, and "tranquilo"—relax. In other words, this is a culture that's generally easygoing and happy, and wants you to act the same. Top it all off with the almost perpetual sunshine, palm trees, the beach and the food.

If you manage to book a table at Tickets, you'll soon find out why the restaurant is so popular

Poblenou
Constant Change

The former fishing village became the centre of Catalan industry during the 19th century. In 1992 it was again transformed by the Olympics, and has lately been rediscovered by start-ups and artists

| Culture | **Cultural Fabric** |

Poblenou was an industrial hub away from the city centre. Today, crumbling textile factories are being remodeled for a new generation of techies and startups in the strategic 22@ innovation district, the city's local urban renewal project. Dilapidated buildings are being renovated as exhibition spaces for architectural firms, art galleries, and design studios, giving the neighborhood a raw, modern edge. To check what's happening in the art scene, visit *Barcelona Culture World*, an art and lounge bar, comprising a gallery that features artists every month and a showroom where designers display their goods. The lounge bar also serves delicious Catalan food. *La Plataforma* is an art gallery that exhibits and sells books, furniture, graphic materials, toys and other wares—all in the name of good design. It's also a production studio and a space for creative minds to share their artistic passions. Even the building itself—an old printing press—is shot through with artistic credentials. *La Escocesa* (pictured), an old textile factory, is an audiovisual production studio, providing artists with affordable spaces to showcase their creations. Check out its exhibition hall, *Espai M*, which features every month the work of an emerging artist.
• Poblenou, various locations, see Index p. 67

Hey, Try This

Opened in 1912, the history of this orxata (tiger nut milk) and ice cream shop spans five generations. This corner shop was named *Tio Ché* ("Uncle Hey") because founding father Joan told local neighbors, "Xe, prova" ("Hey, try this"). Flavours include coffee, cream and meringued milk but those looking for an extra lift could go for Baileys, whisky or rum. Some indoor seating is available, but it's not as fun as having your cool beverages on the vibrant strip, Rambla de Poblenou. Expect long queues in the summer—and tables fill fast.
• El Tío Ché, Rambla de Poblenou 44, Poblenou, eltioche.es

Culture   **Space and Lines**

Understated museum *Can Framis* intrigues with its minimalist façade. Originally a factory built as the 18th century wound to a close, it was converted a few years back into a museum of contemporary art with over 300 works from modern Catalan creators. Parts of the historic building are maintained, while other parts are renovated and modern. There's nothing flashy about it—the open spaces and ample light let you focus on the art. If you're looking for a bookshop or café, you won't find one. The museum is designed to be a space where art takes centre stage.
• Can Framis Museum, Carrer Roc Boronat 116-126, Poblenou, fundaciovilacasas.com

Food   **Down-To-Earth**

Serving traditional Spanish tapas, *El 58* also provides delicious, innovative variations with a French or Asian twist that still manage to taste authentic. The food here is made with fresh, seasonal ingredients—and you can tell from the flavour. Starring dishes include hummus, aubergine with honey and fried potatoes with sun-dried tomatoes and allioli. Ask if you can dine in the back—the charm of the restaurant is in its quaint courtyard. It's a versatile place to have lunch during the day with family or sip vermouth in the evening with friends. Either way, it feels like home.
• El 58, Rambla de Poblenou, 58, Poblenou

Form and Function

One of the latest additions to the city's cultural life, the new *Barcelona Design Museum* was formed by merging the collections of four museums, across product, fashion and graphic design. Its collection covers 400 AD to the present, and the Documentation Centre contains more than 22,000 documents comprising books, magazines and contemporary and historic graphic material. The building was designed by the MBM team of architects and textures the Poblenou with yet another iconic piece of architecture.
• Museu del Disseny de Barcelona, Plaça de les Glòries Catalanes 37, museudeldisseny.cat

Food **Neighbourhood Delicacy**

This decades-old restaurant sits on a pedestrianised street and is famed as a treasure of Poblenou. The old, well-stocked wine shop next door is run by the owner's brother; the food-wine synergy of the bar and bodega keeps locals coming back. The restaurant itself is cosy and small, but the food packs amazing flavour. The menu includes calamares, potato-filled dumplings and snails. Perhaps the most popular choice is Cantabrian anchovies with sun-dried tomatoes served on a slice of bread. High quality, moderately priced—and above all, delicious.
• La Pubilla del Taulat, Carrer de Marià Aguiló 131, Poblenou, pubilladeltaulat.com

Night **Throwback**

If the façade of this corner bar looks like an old drugstore, that's because it was. Reminiscent of the 1950s, the bar's specialties are cocktails and vermouths. The sophisticated, sleek and elegant interior has retro-style leather booths and chrome bar stools to give it that cool, vintage feel. As for the food, they proudly serve guilt-free local and ecological products such as sausage with chickpeas or tuna marmite. Expect to pay a little more for drinks—but the value is woven into the charming, classy ambiance.
• Balius Bar, Carrer de Pujades, 196, Poblenou

Culture Vamos a la Playa

Poblenou is bordered by three beaches: Bogatell, Mar Bella, and Nova Mar Bella. Just walking along the connected boardwalk, you're bound to see the xiringuitos, or bars on the sand, blaring chillout beats through their speakers. *Mar Bella Beach* has attractions for each member of the family: a children's playground, a skate park and a boardwalk for bikers and pedestrians. The seafood restaurants of *Nova Mar Bella* sit at a higher altitude providing a spectacular view of the waterfront and the passers-by. Come early for a delicious weekend morning breakfast, as restaurants tend to fill up on sunny days. *Xiringuito Escribà* has a variety of rice dishes such as black rice, fideuà (Catalan noodles) and paella. Try the fresh seafood: grilled Galician razor clams or mussels a la marinière. *Catamaran*, its close neighbour on the same row, also serves a glorious paella in its pan with just the right amount of "socorrat", the crispy crust at the bottom. Hit up *Base Nautica Bar* if you're looking to skip a full meal. Here, you can opt for a small tapa of olives and a strong drink while basking in the heat and watching the sun-lovers stroll by.

• Poblenou, various locations, see Index p. 67

Zosen Bandido & Mina Hamada, Artists

Off the Beaten Path

<u>Zosen Bandido & Mina Hamada</u>
They are lovers, artists and collaborators. When they work on a piece of art together, it's nearly impossible to tell who did what, as their handwritings seem to meld. While their works are a colourful explosion, the picture that emerges exhibits a special reluctance. Though complementary in their art, their backgrounds couldn't be more different. Zosen moved with his family from Argentina to Barcelona when he was about 12 years old, while US-born Mina grew up in Japan and initially planned to live in the Spanish city for only one year

Zosen and Mina live in Sants, Barcelona's largest district, but their studios are located on the other side of the city centre, in Poblenou. Their daily commute takes them past everything the city has to offer, from crowded urban areas to the remote neighbourhoods where Catalans go about their usual business. Here, the couple takes us on a tour of their favourite places in Barcelona, including the secret spots that, to this day, have remained well off the beaten path

Zosen, what is so appealing about Barcelona?

Zosen: Barcelona is my base. Although I'm not Catalan, it kind of feels like I am from here. I tried other cities such as Berlin, for example, but I came back.

Are these the same reasons that brought you here, Mina?

Mina: Before I came here as part of my one-year grant, I had only been to Barcelona for one day when I travelled around Europe with my mum. I decided to come here and stay longer as I liked the atmosphere of the city and the fact that it is so close to the sea.

Today you are both residents. Where is your studio located?

Mina: In Poblenou.

Zosen: It's, let's say, the Catalan Manchester—it was built for working. Since the late 1990s, this has changed. Our studio was once a factory, too. I came to this neighbourhood for the first time as a teenager, when I was painting graffiti. The factories offered many empty walls and there were even some walls that were approved for being painted—so-called Hall of Fames. So I've known this area for quite a long time and was able to observe the changes.

Is the city of Barcelona a source of inspiration for your art?

Zosen: Yes, definitely, as I grew up here. I was involved in different movements like skateboarding, hip-hop, hardcore punk... I think the inspiration actually happens unconsciously: I remember situations about 15 years ago when graffiti writers from other cities or countries were saying that graffiti in Barcelona looked so different from other places. Now, in times of the internet, it's all mingled and kind of the same anywhere. But

then they said it was the use of colours that made the difference. I don't exactly know why it has been like this, but I can imagine that growing up in a Mediterranean flavour surrounded by art from Miró and architecture by Gaudí does something to you.

Mina: I think my art has become freer since I've been living in Barcelona. In comparison to Japanese culture, where people try to conform, people here demonstrate whenever they feel mistreated or misunderstood. When I lived in Japan, my paintings looked like the dark side of me coming out. This completely changed here. The colours I am using are the best proof of this.

Talking about neighbourhoods, are there any nice ones that still have a local vibe?

Mina: Gràcia. It's very calm and cosy. If you go there in August, you will be mesmerised by the beautiful decorations on the street. They are made for the summer party that takes place in the second week of August each year.

Zosen: True. The decorations are prepared all year long by the neighbours that are into it.

Mina: I was awed when I was at the fiesta for the first time, because of the beauty but also because there are all generations celebrating together. You will see children on the street until late at night.

Is the area also worth visiting when there isn't a summer party going on?

Zosen: Definitely. Especially for all the many nice, small independent shops. Actually, there is always more than one thing happening. Artists have their studios there and open them to the public.

Mina: *Meublé* is also a good and nice example of this multidisciplinary approach. It's a shop for

Get lost in a green vision of Barclona at the Parc del Laberint

vintage furniture, but they also sell some selected vintage fashion, and it's also an exhibition and workshop space.

What is it like in Sants, the neighbourhood where you live?
Zosen: It's a Catalan neighbourhood, very homey. Many old people who maybe even grew up there are still living in this area.
Mina: You can find the old Barcelona there.

Speaking of food, where in Barcelona do you get the best breakfast?
Zosen: My sisters run *El Rincon de Melissa*. The food is Mediterranean with some Argentinian influences—empanadas, tarts and cakes are on the menu. And *Pizzas l'Àvia* is great. The owner is from Uruguay and he mixes his home cuisine with Catalan. And there is *Lukumas*. You will get the best doughnuts and bagels there. The guy running it is from Greece. He

just opened his second store. One is in Gracia and another one is downtown.
Mina: And there is one very special coffee shop that is actually more a theatre. It is called *Antic Teatre*. They have a garden where you can have your coffee. And it's in the centre of Barcelona. And I can tell you, there are not many green oases like this.

Where do you recommend for dinner?
Zosen: *Chen Ji*. It's a Chinese restaurant but not a Chinese restaurant for Western people. It's Chinese food for Chinese people. It's currently being discovered by more and more people for its quality.
Mina: And I love tapas. You will get the best at *Bar Ramón*.

Are there any good markets selling fresh fruits and vegetables?
Zosen: The most famous one is probably *La Boqueria*. It's a tourist

Studiostore knows every child is an artist—the problem is staying an artist when you grow up

attraction, but it's also really good. If you go there you should go all the way through to the stalls and reach the ones that are furthest away from Las Ramblas. The prices get lower the further you go.

Mina: If you just go there to get a snack during the day, I recommend enjoying it at Parc de la Ciutadella—it's a park close by the market.

Zosen: True. It's a nice, nearby recreational area. It's big and you can find a nice quiet spot. You will probably have the impression that it looks kind of unreal. It reminds of the perfection of an amusement park and that's exactly what it once was at the beginning of the 20th century. And if you are at Ciutadella, make sure you go to *Studiostore*, too. It's a mix of shop, gallery and studio.

What about a green sanctuary outside the city centre?
Zosen: I love the *Parc del*

Laberint d'Horta. It's Barcelona's oldest park and an amazing maze. It's at the hillside of Serra de Collserola—maybe some 25 minutes by subway from the centre. And there is the Montserrat Mountains. It's beautiful. You can go hiking or visit the Benedictine monastery, *Santa Maria*.

If you had visitors for a weekend, which spots would you take them to?
Mina: *La Sagrada Família* is a must see as well as the *Joan Miró Foundation*. And I go to the *Park Guell* with everybody who visits me. In the morning you will have a nice view of the sun rising.

Zosen: And a visit to *CCCB* will be on the schedule. It has a nice program: exhibitions, dance performances. It's a formal place, but very open-minded at the same time.

Recuerdos

Hecho a Mano

Made in Barcelona, handcrafted and finished in sunny colours—the collection of Emma Pardos reflects the city's heartbeat. Her small cotton bag is a functional companion for wandering between Rambla and the beach.

• Emma Pardos, emmapardos.com

Walk like a Catalan

Handmade for the summer breeze, these primary colours will make your feet feel airy and light. The Catalan's shoe of choice.

• Maians, maians.es

Dream Team

The revival of Vermouth is celebrated in Bodegas all over Barcelona. Bar Bodega Quimet in Gràcia offers some of the finest. This particular one comes with an eye catching Geiser soda bottle for a reasonable price. Check-in luggage recommended...

• Bar Bodega Quimet

Books

Joan Colom: Les Gens Du Raval
• Joan Colom, 2006

Time travel: Colom spent nearly every weekend with his camera in the 1950s in Raval—the now hip district which was wild and dangerous in those days. Intimate observations in black and white.

Barça: A People's Passion
• Jimmy Burns, 2000

FC Barcelona is much more than a football club—it is a social phenomenon. Though at first sight Burns's book is about football, buried beneath is the story of more than a hundred years of obsessive Catalan pride.

An Olympic Death,
• Manuel Vázquez Montalbán, 1994

A fine example of European "noir" literature—set in the unstable times of the Olympiad in Barcelona at the beginning of the 1990s. Detective Pepe Carvalho is back in action: drinking, eating, fighting and romancing.

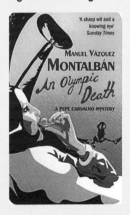

Movies

All About My Mother
• Pedro Almodóvar, 1999

Almodóvar's classic and a winner of several awards. This comedy-drama has all the ingredients its director is famous for: a great cast, a labyrinthine plot and a set full of bright colours and flashy art.

Barcelona
• Whit Stillman, 1994

Following the anti-American movement in Europe in the late 1980s, this comedy follows two Americans, a soldier and an uptight businessman through bars, discos and interactions with Catalan women.

Biutiful
• Alejandro González Iñárritu, 2010

The story of a single father raising two children while juggling the Chinese sweatshop he runs and the Senegalese who sell his goods. A brilliant glimpse into the darker side of the Catalan city.

Music

Un Altre Jo
•Guillamino & The Control Z's, 2013

Guillamino is a Barcelona-based musical multi-talent. With "Guillamino & The Control Z's" he releases Catalan hip hop spiced with funk, Latin and jazz. Another project "Olde Gods" highlights his club-land side—check out Soundcloud for his DJ work.

Alenar
• Maria del Mar Bonet, 1977

Born in Mallorca del Mar, Bonet moved to Barcelona in 1967 and soon got in touch with iconic musical project "Els Setze Jutges", a major voice for the Catalan independence movement. Her 1977 Album "Alenar" merges smooth compositions with big feelings and a great voice to top it all.

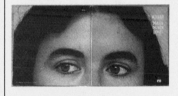

Duquende y la guitarra de Tomatito
• Duquende, 1993

Juan Cortés "Duquende" is the great Gypsy voice of today's Catalan flamenco. His debut album is a well-rounded soundtrack for an intense weekend in town full of everything that makes life here so enjoyable.

The Serras

History and art come together majestically at The Serras on Barcelona's celebrated Passeig de Colom. Here, breezes blow off the Mediterranean into large rooms with balconies that offer a front row seat to this trendy Barcelona neighborhood. Here too can be found a top Catalan chef and the site of Pablo Picasso's first studio where he painted "Ciencia y Caridad" in 1897. Today, a new masterpiece is being created in the form of a stylish rooftop terrace, spacious rooms with tiles echoing the classic Barcelona style and a historic façade by a famous 19th-century architect—all combined with the latest technological and luxury facilities to create a truly hassle-free environment.

Grand Hotel Central

The Grand Hotel Central offers a discreet and luxurious hideaway amid the bustle of Barcelona's fashionable El Born district. Owner Pau Guardans has completely reworked a 1920s building to create a hotel that evokes the splendor of Barcelona's high society in the early part of the 20th century. The result is a tranquil property infused with timeless elegance and urban soul. Guardans' reputation as a trendsetter and visionary is evident in the finer details of the hotel. With his very own city guide "Barcelona Around", Guardans offers guests an insider view of this vibrant city.

Hotel Granados 83

An oasis of zen tranquility in the heart of the Old City, Hotel Granados 83 brings a touch of New York industrial-chic to Barcelona. The glass, steel, and exposed brick of the hotel's airy interiors combine with hotel owner Jordi Clos' personal collection of original Hindu and Buddhist artworks dating from as early as the 10th century. The result? An urban getaway as soothing as it is inspiring. True to both location and inspiration, the hotel's restaurant offers sublime Mediterranean and Asian fusion.

Story

The Porter

For Francisco González Ledesma

*"Manager of hydroelectric company disappears."
H.F.P., the financial vice-president of ENHER, went
missing from his family home on Christmas Eve. The
search has been complicated by the heavy snowfall in
Barcelona, which has left Sant Esteve unrecognisable.
The director is described as being 1.50 metres tall, 57
kilos, dark-skinned with a black moustache and was
wearing a dark suit, dark grey coat and bowler hat
at the time of his disappearance. It is well known that
H.F.P. has been the staunchest advocate of building
a skyscraper on the site of the old Hotel Fuster.*
—La Vanguardia, 27.12.1962

Like a spot of dirt in the snow, those two tiles at the
entrance of the old Hotel Fuster had spent half a
century bothering people. It all began at Christmas
1962, the year when a massive snowstorm ravaged
the city. They say the accident was the product of
an unforgivable oversight, a sample of indecent
clumsiness. A labourer dropped a pallet of potted
poinsettias, intended for New Year's Eve.

The façade of the Casa Fuster was the first in
Barcelona made out completely of white marble. The
marble was of the highest quality. It had been brought
expressly from Carrera for the occasion. The floor
was waxed with care every day. It was polished to
look like a mirror. So much so that sometimes the
reflection made people feel dizzy. But nobody told this
to the labourer who moved the pallet to the ball-
rooms. So the man slipped, stumbled with the wooden
tables and scattered the hotel entrance with pot
shards. Two precious, irreplaceable tiles, which had
been there for forty years, were shattered. All for
a few poinsettias which would not even last a month.

It all happened at dawn. There were no witnesses
to the accident. At least, that was the story given
to the papers by the new owners of the building: the
National Hydroelectric Company of Ribagorçana.
It was like adding vinegar to a paper cut, because
word had spread that the company wanted to sell
the Fuster to erect a skyscraper. And the Passeig de
Gràcia, the neighbourhood itself and the entire city
of Barcelona had been walking around sharpening

knives for months. So anger became confusion and
when the hotel manager tried to explain, he failed
to convince anyone.

To crown it all, nobody kicked out the bandy-
legged fool, the incompetent one, that Albert
Agramunt, the self-confessed marble-slayer. Not only
was he not thrown into the street like a dog, but
he was offered the post of porter for life. A bloke
who had nothing to do with the hotel business, who
had hitherto only been known for hanging around
at Barcelona dock and who had been rumoured
to have done time in prison in Sicily.

Faced with criticism, the director of ENHER argued
that, far from being a reward, this was the worst pun-
ishment imaginable. It would be shame taken to
infinity. There, Agramunt would come face to face with
the repulsion which his awkwardness would undoubt-
edly generate in the following generations of guests
and visitors. He would have to endure the embarrass-
ment of feeling himself glared at day after day by
locals and foreigners. And to make matters worse, he
would never be able to remove that oppressive uniform—come rain or shine, dictatorship or democracy,
not even if Barça won five consecutive cups.

But that wasn't what the vigilante's expression
said. Fifty years later there was no hesitation in his
eyes. There was no shame in his mouth. His hands
never begged forgiveness for the heresy committed
against the floor of the facade.

Every Christmas Eve the smell of myrrh sprouts
from these two tiles, from the hundred and fifty centi-
metres of jet-black slate and the porter at the Hotel
Fuster smiles. With his gold-edged uniform buttoned
to the neck and royal purple boots.

*José Louis Correa is a Spanish professor of literature
and a writer. Detective Ricardo Blanco is the protago-
nist of his famous series of crime novels, with "Blue
Christmas" the latest. Among Correa's several awards
are included the Premio Benito Pérez Armas and the
Premio Vargas Llosa*

Available from LOST iN

Next Issue: Ibiza

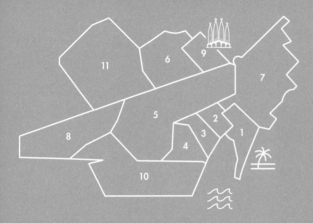

Districts

1/ Barcelo-neta

Baluard
Carrer del Baluart 38
+34 93 221 12 08
baluardbarceloneta
.com → p.23 Ⓕ

Barraca
Passeig Marítim
Barceloneta 1
+34 93 224 12 53
→ p.46 Ⓕ

Kaiku
Plaza del Mar 1
+34 93 221 90 82
restaurantkaiku.cat
→ p.46 Ⓕ

La Cova Fumada
Carrer del Baluart 56
+34 93 221 40 61
→ p.16 Ⓝ

**Mercat de la
Barceloneta**
Plaça de la Font 1
+34 93 221 64 71
mercatdelabarcelo
neta.com → p.17 Ⓕ, Ⓞ

**The Only Fish
in the Sea**
Carrer de
l'Atlàntida 47
+34 93 611 37 98
→ p.25 Ⓢ

Subwax
Marques d. l. Mina 2
+34 63 314 89 83
subwaxbcn.com
→ p.31 Ⓢ

2/El Born

About Arianne
Carrer de l'Esquirol 5
+34 69 278 40 92
aboutarianne.com
→ p.21 Ⓢ

Antic Teatre
Carrer de Verdaguer
i Callís 12
+34 93 315 23 54
anticteatre.com
→ p.54 Ⓕ

Bar del Pla
Carrer Montcada 2
+34 93 268 30 03
bardelpla.cat
→ p.18 Ⓝ

Bar Mundial
Plaza Sant Agustí
Vell 1
+34 93 319 90 56
→ p.15, 16 Ⓝ

Bar Pasajes
Carrer de Sant Pere
Més Alt 31
+34 93 310 55 35
→ p.15 Ⓝ

**Basílica Santa Maria
del Mar**
Plaça Santa Maria 1
+34 93 310 23 90
santamariadelmar
barcelona.org
→ p.14 Ⓒ

Bon Vent
Carrer de
l'Argenteria 41
+34 93 295 40 53
bonvent.cat
→ p.19 Ⓕ

Colmillo de Morsa
Carrer de Vic 15
colmillodemorsa.com
→ p.17, 24 Ⓢ

Cuines Santa Caterina
Av. de Francesc
Cambó 16
+34 93 268 99 18
→ p.46 Ⓕ

Espai Mescladís
Carrer Carders 35
+34 93 319 87 32
mescladis.org
→ p.19 Ⓕ

Guzzo
Plaça Comercial 10
+34 93 667 00 36
guzzo.es
→ p.20 Ⓕ, Ⓒ, Ⓝ

Ivori
Carrer Mirallers 7
+34 65.750 00 41
ivoribarcelona.com
→ p.17, Ⓢ

La Estrella
Carrer d'Ocata 6
+34 93 310 27 68
→ p.15, Ⓕ

La Paradeta
Carrer Comercial 7
+34 93 268 19 39
laparadeta.com
→ p.19 Ⓕ

La Tercera
Carrer Brosolí 4
latercerashop.com
→ p.17 Ⓢ

Maian Coquette
Carrer del Rec 65
+34 93 319 29 76
coquettebcn.com
→ p.21 Ⓢ

Meneghina
Carrer Tiradors 2
+34 93 119 22 21
→ p.25 Ⓕ

Mosquito Tapas
Carrer Carders 46
+34 93 268 75 69
mosquitotapas.com
→ p.20 Ⓕ

**Museu de Cultures
del Món**
Carrer Montcada 12
+34 93 256 23 00
museCulturesmon.bcn
→ p.17 Ⓒ

Natalie Capell
Carrer de la
Carassa 2
+34 93 319 92 19
nataliecapell.com
→ p.21 Ⓢ

**Palau de la Música
Catalana**
Palau Música 4-6
+34 93 295 72 00
palaumusica.org
→ p.14 Ⓒ

Picasso Museum
Carrer
Montcada 15–23
+34 93 256 30 00
museupicasso.bcn
→ p.14, 17 ©

Pony
Portal Nou 23
+34 60 549 06 98
→ p.15 Ⓝ

Room
Carrer Flassaders 31
+34 93 268 96 55
room-mr.com
→ p.21 Ⓢ

Studiostore
Calle Comerç 17
+34 93 2 22 50 75
studiostore.es
→ p.55 Ⓢ

3/El Gòtic

El Bombón
La Mercè 13
+34 93 310 76 99
→ p.31 Ⓝ

Koy Shunka
Copons 7
+34 93 412 79 39
koyshunka.com
→ p.25 Ⓕ

4/El Raval

**360° Terrace at
Hotel Barceló Raval**
Rambla del Raval
17–21
→ p.46 Ⓝ

Bar 33/45
Carrer de Joaquín
Costa 4
+34 93 187 41 38
3345.struments.com
→ p.32 Ⓕ

Bar Calders
Carrer Parlament 25
+34 93 329 93 49
→ p.16 Ⓝ

Bar Lobo
Carrer del Pintor
Fortuny 3
+34 93 481 53 46
→ p.46 Ⓝ, Ⓕ

Betty Ford's
Carrer de Joaquín
Costa 56
+34 93 304 13 68
→ p.15 Ⓕ

Casa Almirall
Joaquín Costa 33
+34 93 318 99 17
casaalmirall.com
→ p.46 Ⓝ

CCCB
Montalegre 5
+34 93 306 41 00
cccb.org → p.55 ©

**Centre d'Art Santa
Mònica**
Les Rambles 7
+34 93 567 11 10
artssantamonica.cat
→ p.31 ©

Discos Paradiso
Carrer Ferlandina 39
+34 93 329 64 40
→ p.31 Ⓝ

Foxy Bar
Carrer de la Riera
Alta 59
+34 93 180 60 04
wearefoxy.com
→ p.31 Ⓝ

La Central
Carrer d'Elisabets 6
+34 90 288 49 90
lacentral.com
→ p.17 Ⓢ

Les Topettes
Carrer de Joaquín
Costa 33
+34 93 500 55 64
lestopettes.com
→ p.24 Ⓢ

Llibreria Calders
Passatge Pere
Calders 9
+34 93 442 78 31
→ p.25 Ⓢ

MACBA
Plaça dels Àngels 1
+34 93 412 08 10
macba.cat → p.17 ©

**Mercat de la
Boqueria**
Les Rambles 91
→ p.17, 54 Ⓕ

Moog Club
Carrer de l'Arc
del Teatre 3
+34 93 319 17 89
masimas.com
→ p.31 Ⓝ

Múltiplos
Calle Lleó 6, local 2
→ p.17 Ⓢ

Nuovum
Carrer del Pintor
Fortuny 30
+34 66 761 29 55
→ p.17 Ⓢ

Pizzas l'Àvia
Calle de la Cera 33
+34 93 442 00 97
→ p.54 Ⓕ

Wah Wah Records
Carrer de la Riera
Baixa 14
+34 93 442 37 03
wah-wahsupersonic.
com → p.31 Ⓝ

5/Eixample

ADN Galeria
Carrer Enric
Granados 49
+34 93 451 00 64
adngaleria.com
→ p.23 ©

Bar Ramón
Carrer del Comte
Borrell 81
+34 93 325 02 83
barramon.com
→ p.54 Ⓕ

Casa Martino
Carrer de Manso 1
+34 93 170 80 96
casamartino.es
→ p.45 Ⓝ

Cerveceria Catalana
Carrer Mallorca 236
+34 93 216 03 68
→ p.45 Ⓕ

Ceviche 103
Carrer Londres 103
+34 93 209 88 35
ceviche103.com
→ p.45 Ⓕ

Chen Ji
Carrer d'Alí Bei 65
+34 93 247 68 31
→ p.54 Ⓕ

Colmado
Carrer Provença 236
+34 93 546 20 06
colmadobarcelona.
com → p.17 Ⓕ

Cosmo
Enric Granados 3
+34 93 453 70 07
galeriacosmo.com
→ p.15 Ⓕ, ©

Gresca
Calle Provença 230
+34 93 451 61 93
gresca.net → p.25 Ⓕ

Hoja Santa
Av. de Mistral 54
+34 93 348 21 92
hojasanta.es
→ p.45 Ⓕ

Jaime Beriestain
Carrer Pau Claris 167
+34 93 515 07 79
beriestain.com
→ p.10 Ⓢ, Ⓕ

La Casa Batllo
Passeig de Gràcia 43
+34 93 216 03 06
casabatllo.es
→ p.23 ©

Madam PumPum
Carrer Bonavista 16
+34 93 457 34 64
madampumpum.com
→ p.17 Ⓢ

MiiN Korean
Carrer Pau Claris 110
+34 93 348 43 94
miin-cosmetics.com
→ p.25 Ⓢ

Morro Fi
Carrer del Consell
de Cent 171
morrofi.cat
→ p.16, 45 Ⓕ

Raïm 1886
Carrer del Progrés 48
+34 93 453 59 58
→ p.14 Ⓝ

Tamarindo
Carrer Aragó 236
+34 93 002 37 74
→ p.45 Ⓕ

Tapas 24
Carrer de la
Diputació 269
+34 93 488 09 77
tapas24.ca
→ p.45 Ⓕ

Taperia Lolita
Carrer Tamarit 104
+34 93 424 52 31
lolitataperia.com
→ p.45 Ⓕ

Tickets Bar
Avinguda del
Parallel 164
ticketsbar.es
→ p.46 Ⓝ, Ⓕ

ON THE ROAD

The App for the Discerning Traveller

Explore insider recommendations and create your personal itinerary with handpicked locations tailored to your desires. Our selection of experiences ranges from independent boutiques, galleries, neighborhood bars to brand new restaurants. Experience a new city from within.

LOST iN